FAMOUS MOVIE MONSTERS™

INTRODUCING

MAD SCIENTISTS

The Rosen Publishing Group, Inc.,
New York

BETTY BURNETT

To Misha

Published in 2007 by The Rosen Publishing Group, Inc.
29 East 21st Street, New York, NY 10010

First Edition

Library of Congress Cataloging-in-Publication Data

Burnett, Betty.
Introducing mad scientists/Betty Burnett.—1st ed.
p. cm.—(Famous movie monsters)
Filmography: p.
Includes bibliographical references and index.
ISBN 1-4042-0827-5 (library binding)
1. Mad scientist films–History and criticism. I. Title. II. Series.
PN1995.9.M2B97 2006
791.43'636—dc22

2005037510

Manufactured in Malaysia

On the cover: Dr. Frankenstein (Colin Clive) at work in his laboratory in 1931's *Frankenstein.*

CONTENTS

CHAPTER 1

THE MAD SCIENTIST IN THE LABORATORY

The mad scientist is a classic movie character. When people think of mad scientists, they think of lunatics with wild hair who shriek with laughter while mixing mysterious potions in secret laboratories.

In the movies, mad scientists generally use science for evil, concocting potions that change people into monsters, inventing death rays, or creating terrible hybrids of human beings and animals. Mad scientists always want to twist nature, changing themselves, others, or the environment in horrible ways. They work alone in hidden laboratories or with the help of equally mad assistants who do their bidding.

Driven to accomplish their goals at any cost, mad scientists often sow the seeds of their own destruction. They may want to take over the world and control people or some aspect of nature. Blinded by their ambition, they pursue their mad creations without any regard for others and often do not realize how evil their mad pursuits are. In many films, mad scientists experiment on themselves, often with disastrous results.

THE STORY OF *DR. JEKYLL AND MR. HYDE* (1931)

A rich, respected medical doctor living in nineteenth-century London, Dr. Henry Jekyll has everything a man could want. He has many friends and is well liked by everyone he meets. However, Dr. Jekyll is also very curious about human nature— and his curiosity eventually destroys him.

Dr. Jekyll wants to know what it feels like to be completely evil and to have no conscience telling him what is good or bad. He wants to do exactly what he feels like doing, whenever he wants to do it, even if it means killing other people.

Dr. Jekyll (Fredric March) holds the chemical concoction that will turn him into Mr. Hyde in 1931's *Dr. Jekyll and Mr. Hyde.* Fredric March would become famous for portraying Dr. Jekyll and his evil alter ego. Although many other actors played the mad doctor, March's portrayal of Jekyll remains the definitive one.

Dr. Jekyll cannot bring himself to become truly evil. Instead, he wants to become someone else, a monster that is capable of committing ghastly deeds he himself wouldn't dare to do. Dr. Jekyll is rich enough to have his own laboratory in his house. In his laboratory, he can shut out the outside world and concentrate on his chemical experiments. Dr. Jekyll makes a number of very strange chemical concoctions. When he is sure he has a good mixture, he drinks it to see how it affects his brain.

Finally, Dr. Jekyll discovers a formula that will turn him into a complete monster. He names this monster Edward Hyde. Mr. Hyde is Dr. Jekyll's "evil twin." When Dr. Jekyll becomes Mr. Hyde, his entire personality transforms. Even his physical appearance changes, becoming grotesque and apelike. Dr. Jekyll creates a whole life for Hyde, complete with a separate apartment and bank account. All of Dr. Jekyll's friends dislike the monstrous Hyde.

Eventually, Dr. Jekyll realizes that Mr. Hyde can be dangerous. He tries to stop himself from transforming into Hyde but finds that he can't. Hyde is now a part of him and no longer needs chemicals to come out and take control.

One evening Hyde is walking down a London street. A man walking toward him seems to take the right of way. This enrages Hyde, who beats the man to death with Jekyll's walking stick. Jekyll realizes that he will be caught. He writes a long letter to his friend and attorney, explaining everything, and then he kills himself.

OTHER VERSIONS OF *DR. JEKYLL AND MR. HYDE*

The novel *The Strange Case of Dr. Jekyll and Mr. Hyde* (1886) was written by Robert Louis Stevenson, the famous author of adventure stories like *Treasure Island* and *Kidnapped*. Since then, at least fifty movies have been made using the Jekyll and Hyde characters.

Fredric March, wearing the makeup of the hideous Mr. Hyde, shocked audiences in 1931 with his apelike appearance. In the movie, Dr. Jekyll made a number of arrangements for his alter ego, such as finding him a place to live. This version of *Dr. Jekyll and Mr. Hyde* was the first with spoken dialogue and sound—previous versions of the film had been silent.

The first movie adaptation of *Dr. Jekyll and Mr. Hyde* was only fifteen minutes long and was made in 1910. Other Jekyll and Hyde films followed in 1912, 1913, and 1920.

However, most critics consider the best film adaptation of Stevenson's novel to be the 1931 version directed by Rouben Mamoulian and starring Fredric March. An outstanding actor, March won an Academy Award for his portrayal of the mad doctor and his alter ego. *Dr. Jekyll and Mr. Hyde* was one of the first films to depict a human being who becomes a monster by drinking a chemical formula. Since then, there have been a number of movies that show scientists experimenting on themselves.

Some of the other actors who have played the demanding double role of Dr. Jekyll and Mr. Hyde are Spencer Tracy, Michael Caine, Mark Redfield, and John Malkovich. The film *Mary Reilly* (1996), starring Julia Roberts, tells the story of Jekyll and Hyde from the point of view of Dr. Jekyll's maid. Matt Keeslar played the famous mad scientist in 2004. In this version of the story, Jekyll is a cancer researcher who creates a computer-generated Hyde, who turns on Jekyll and kills him.

Many of the film versions differ widely from Stevenson's original story. Some add material that was not in the story, such as a romantic interest, or manipulate the plot to create greater suspense. But there is one scene that appears in nearly every version made for the screen: the handsome Dr. Jekyll holds a glass of foaming potion to his lips, hesitates for a moment, shakes off his doubt, and drinks the glass down. Suddenly, a look of horror crosses his face. He reels from the effects of the drink. Gradually his hands change into hairy claws, his face is trans-formed by anger, and his straight back stoops into an ugly hunch. He roars with satisfaction and leaves his house to wreak havoc.

THE STORY OF *THE INVISIBLE MAN* (1933)

At the turn of the twentieth century, British scientist Dr. Jack Griffin discovers that a drug called monocaine will make him invisible. Griffin thinks that being invisible will allow him to act as he pleases. He can spy on people, scare them, and steal things without getting caught.

It isn't long before Griffin's dream of invisibility becomes a nightmare. The monocaine begins to drive him insane. He is desperate to find an antidote before something terrible happens.

Griffin goes to a remote village, where he rents a room in a boarding house. Wearing bandages around his face, dark glasses, a fake beard, and gloves to cover his hands, Griffin hopes that no one will discover his terrible secret. Griffin no longer looks like a normal man—in fact, he no longer looks like anything at all.

One night, the invisible Griffin walks through the countryside. The moon goes behind a cloud. Driven mad by monocaine, he thinks the moon is hiding from him. He cries out, "Power! To make the whole world grovel at my feet, to walk into the gold vaults of nations, the chambers of kings . . . Even the moon is frightened of me, frightened to death."

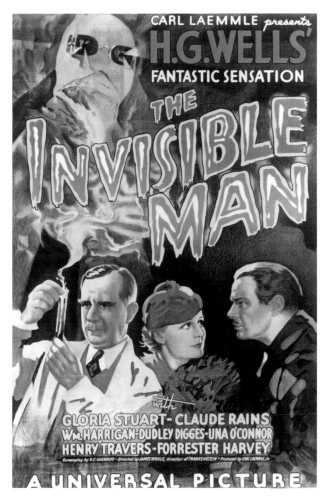

A movie poster announced the release of *The Invisible Man* in 1933. The scientist on the bottom left is examining a test tube that no doubt contains an invisibility potion.

Completely covered by bandages, dark glasses, gloves, and clothing, Claude Rains portrays the doomed Dr. Griffin in 1933's *The Invisible Man*. A few moments after this scene, he disrobes and disappears, confounding the policeman and villagers who were questioning him about a mysterious murder. On the table in front of him are the vials, bottles, chemicals, and microscope necessary for his experiments.

As Griffin succumbs to madness, he is overcome with uncontrollable fits of murderous rage. He terrorizes the village as an invisible killer. At last, he is tracked down and shot by the police. As Griffin dies, his body finally becomes visible again.

OTHER VERSIONS OF *THE INVISIBLE MAN*

The science fiction writer H. G. Wells wrote *The Invisible Man*, which was published in 1897. Wells wrote a number of famous science fiction novels and stories, including *The War of the Worlds* (1898) and *The Time Machine* (1895). Many of Wells's works have been made into films, but few have been able to match *The Invisible Man*'s eerie atmosphere. Actor Claude Rains played the part of power-hungry Dr. Griffin in Universal Studios' 1933 adaptation of the novel. Although other actors would go on to play Griffin in other versions of the story, Rains's portrayal of the doomed scientist remains the definitive one.

The Invisible Man was directed by James Whale, who also directed *Frankenstein* (1931) and *The Bride of Frankenstein* (1935). Whale brought an artistic sensibility to *The Invisible Man*, making it one of Universal's most iconic movies.

Although *The Invisible Man* was Rains's first Hollywood movie, the audience had to wait until the end of the film to actually see him. Cast for his sophisticated voice and his acting ability, Rains would go on to appear in many classic Hollywood films.

The Invisible Man Returns, directed by Joe May, was released in 1940. In this movie, Griffin's son gives the invisibility serum to a man condemned to death for a murder he didn't commit. Unseen, he escapes prison and finds the real murderer, but then goes mad and dies.

Universal attempted to capitalize on the success of *The Invisible Man Returns* with *The Invisible Woman* (1940). The humorous, slapstick script was much different from the previous two movies in the series. In this film, a department store worker, played by Virginia Bruce, gets fired from her job. She uses an invisibility machine to get revenge on her foul-tempered boss.

Universal's final movie in the series, *Invisible Agent*, was released in 1942, shortly after the United States entered World War II. The screenplay was written by Curt Siodmak, who had previously written scripts for horror and science fiction films such as *The Wolf Man* (1941). In *Invisible Agent*, Dr. Griffin's grandson uses his grandfather's invisibility formula to spy on the Nazis. A Jewish refugee from Nazi-controlled Germany, Siodmak took great pleasure in portraying the Nazis as bumbling fools.

THE STORY OF *THE FLY* (1986)

Scientist Seth Brundle meets journalist Veronica Quaife at a party. He tells her that his scientific work will "change human life as we know it." She doesn't believe him, but Brundle convinces her to visit his lab.

Brundle's warehouse laboratory is located in a deserted part of town. He explains that he's been experimenting with teleportation, or moving matter from one place to another by disassembling the molecules at one place and instantly reassembling them at another. If this works, it will completely change the transportation industry. There will no longer be a need for trucks, cars, or airplanes.

Brundle has a powerful computer and two telepods in his lab. He shows Quaife that he is able to teleport inanimate objects from one telepod to another. His goal is to transport living creatures. Quaife agrees to help Seth videotape the experiments.

Jeff Goldblum portrays an ailing Dr. Seth Brundle in the 1986 movie *The Fly*. **As he begins his transformation into a fly, Brundle develops an insatiable sweet tooth. As his transformation progresses, his skin begins to look diseased and he develops the ability to climb up walls. The special makeup effects for the film shocked viewers at the time of the film's release.**

His first attempt to teleport a live baboon from one telepod to another is a gruesome failure. Brundle figures out what he did wrong and reprograms his computer. The next test is success-ful, and the baboon he teleports seems to be perfectly healthy after the experiment.

Excited by his accomplishment, Brundle decides to teleport himself. He climbs into the telepod, unaware that a fly has entered with him. He teleports himself, and the experiment seems to be successful. Brundle and Quaife celebrate and make plans to publicize the event.

Something strange has begun to happen to Brundle, however. Gradually, he begins to change. He has more energy, craves sugar, and exhibits inhuman strength. Quaife notices strange, stiff hairs growing on his back. Brundle is excited by these changes, but Quaife thinks that something is wrong. She gets the hairs from his back analyzed, and they appear to be insect hairs.

Brundle transforms rapidly. He neglects his laboratory, which soon becomes filthy and fills with garbage. His fingernails begin to fall off. He can no longer chew food, but instead must regurgitate on it in order to liquefy it. He then sucks up the liquefied meal. His skin develops thick, scaly growths. Horrified, he and Quaife realize that he is becoming a giant fly.

The computer controlling the telepods was confused by the fact that Brundle and the fly had different genes. The teleportation process fused the fly's genes with Brundle's. Brundle is a brilliant scientist, but there is nothing he can do to reverse his sickening transformation. As he becomes more and more insectlike, he begins to lose his mind. In a last-ditch effort to regain his humanity, he tries another teleportation experiment—and is killed.

OTHER VERSIONS OF *THE FLY*

Starring Jeff Goldblum as Seth Brundle and Geena Davis as Veronica Quaife, *The Fly* was directed by David Cronenberg. Famous for creating extremely grisly horror films, Cronenberg pulled out all the stops with *The Fly*. *The Fly II* (1989) followed the story of Brundle's son, Martin Brundle (Eric Stolz), who inherits his father's strange genes. Brundle's son is fully grown and mature at the age of five. It isn't long before he begins changing, just like his father did. Unlike his father, Martin Brundle finds a way to reverse the process.

The Fly was a remake of an earlier film with the same name, based on a short story by French writer George Langelaan. The first version of *The Fly*, directed by Kurt Neumann, appeared in 1958. David Hedison was cast as the scientist Andre Delambre, and Vincent Price as his brother François. In the original story, Andre Delambre, like Brundle, is obsessed with his invention, a matter transporter. He decides to transport himself as an experiment. His atoms also become accidentally merged with those of a fly. Rather than turning completely into an insect, Delambre emerges from his experiment with the head and arm of a giant fly. The fly survives the experiment as well, but now it has a tiny human head and arm. Eventually, Delambre is destroyed, and a spider eats the fly.

Return of the Fly followed in 1959. It was directed by Edward Bernds, who had previously directed a number of Three Stooges films. *Return of thc Fly* takes place fifteen years after the events of the first movie. Andre Delambre's son, Philippe Delambre (Brett Halsey), attempts to continue his father's work. Philippe is assisted by his uncle, François (again played by Vincent Price). Unfortunately for Philippe, their experiments end in disaster. Philippe's body is combined with that of a fly—the same fate suffered by his father. A third installment of the series, *Curse of the Fly* (1965), explores thc further misadventures of the Delambre family.

CHAPTER 2

THE MAD SCIENTIST AND MOTHER NATURE

Many mad scientists are not content to stay in their laboratories and experiment only on themselves. Some want to experiment on animals or on other people. They hope to control their environment in some way so they will become powerful. They want people to be so afraid of them that they will submit to insane demands. Others want to go as far as to take over the world, or even destroy it. Sometimes, these mad scientists aren't evil at all, but are simply unaware that their experiments are destructive.

THE STORY OF *ISLAND OF LOST SOULS* (1933)

A shipwrecked man is drifting alone at sea in a raft when he is rescued by a passing boat. The boat, carrying a cargo of animals, is on its way to the island of Dr. Moreau.

An island in the middle of the ocean is a perfect place for a mad scientist's laboratory. The island's isolation protects it from unfriendly visitors. Arrivals are only by invitation—or accident.

Charles Laughton played the mad Dr. Moreau in 1933's *Island of Lost Souls*. Here, he uses a whip to keep the "manimals" under control. Bela Lugosi, famous for his role as Count Dracula in 1931's *Dracula*, had a small part in the film as a manimal. *Island of Lost Souls* was so shocking when it appeared that It was actually banned in England, Laughton's home country.

When he reaches the island, the shipwrecked man is horrified to discover that Dr. Moreau is trying to create hybrids of humans and animals, which he calls manimals, through grisly transplantation surgery. Dr. Moreau carries out his insane surgery in a building known to the manimals as the House of Pain. The manimals are taught a rigid code of behavior to keep them subservient to Dr. Moreau. But when Moreau angers the manimals by instituting stricter rules, they rebel and capture the mad scientist. He meets his end at the hands of his creations in his own notorious House of Pain.

OTHER VERSIONS OF *ISLAND OF LOST SOULS*

Island of Lost Souls was based on H. G. Wells's book *The Island of Dr. Moreau. Island of Lost Souls* starred the British actor Charles Laughton as Dr. Moreau and Bela Lugosi as one of the manimals.

The *Island of Dr. Moreau* has been adapted for the screen several times since *Island of Lost Souls* was released in 1933. In 1977, a version called *The Island of Dr. Moreau* was released with Burt Lancaster playing Moreau; and in 1996 the legendary actor Marlon Brando played the mad scientist. The 1996 version of *The Island of Dr. Moreau* also updated the classic story with an altered plot and digital special effects. In this version, Dr. Moreau creates his manimals by altering their DNA, and he wins their obedience by giving them chemicals and electric shocks.

THE STORY OF *JURASSIC PARK* (1993)

John Hammond is an extremely wealthy man who has purchased a remote island and turned it into a large zoo with prehistoric animals. Hammond is not a scientist himself, but he employs a team of scientists to realize his dream of bringing dinosaurs back to life. Hammond's scientists use genetic manipulation to achieve their goal. They discover that some mosquitoes that fed on dinosaur blood in the Jurassic period were preserved in amber for sixty-five million years. The mosquitoes still have dinosaur blood inside of them. Even one drop of dinosaur blood has enough DNA to recreate a dinosaur embryo in a lab. All Hammond's scientists need to do is extract the blood and use the DNA to make dinosaur embryos.

Hammond is a gentle, grandfatherly man who wants to create an island paradise called Jurassic Park where tourists can see living dinosaurs. He does not want to hide the results of his experiments. He is certain that tourists will flock to Jurassic Park and he'll make a fortune. Because he needs to follow insurance regulations, Hammond asks dinosaur expert Dr. Alan Grant and two other scientists, Dr. Ian Malcolm and Dr. Ellie Sattler, to check out Jurassic Park before it opens. Malcolm is a mathematician who specializes in chaos theory; Sattler is a paleobotanist, or a scientist who studies fossil plants. Malcolm is concerned about the possible dangers posed by the project. He tells Hammond, "The complete lack of humility for nature that's being displayed here is staggering." Malcolm is concerned that Hammond is trying to control nature and will end up paying a price for it.

Hammond insists that the dangerous, meat-eating dinosaurs at Jurassic Park are safely contained within twenty-four-foot-high electric fences. To prove that he is certain the island is secure, Hammond invites his grandchildren Lex and Tim to join them.

Unbeknownst to Hammond, greedy corporations want his dinosaur embryos. The computer expert at Jurassic Park, Dennis Nedry, decides to sell the embryos to the Bisys Corporation. Nedry disables the security system so that he can escape with the stolen embryos. This enables nine dangerous dinosaurs to escape their enclosures.

The mad scientist–like John Hammond, played by Richard Attenborough *(left)*, gloats over the dinosaur eggs that he created in his Jurassic Park. It won't be long before he regrets tampering with nature. Dr. Ellie Sattler (Laura Dern) and Dr. Alan Grant (Sam Neill) gaze in wonder at the eggs, but aren't so sure the dinosaur theme park is a good thing. The first *Jurassic Park* movie appeared in 1993.

Grant and the children escape to the visitors' center, where they think they will be safe. The most dangerous dinosaurs in the park, the intelligent, carnivorous raptors, follow them. The children are trapped in the visitors' center's kitchen by the vicious raptors. They escape the kitchen and are amazed to see a Tyrannosaurus rex approach to attack the raptors, letting them go free. Lex figures out how to restore power to the park, and a helicopter arrives to rescue them.

A MAD SCIENTIST BLOCKBUSTER

Based on Michael Crichton's 1990 novel of the same name, *Jurassic Park* appeared in movie theaters in 1993. A number of Crichton's best-selling novels have been adapted into films, such as the *The Andromeda Strain* (1971), *Congo* (1995), and *Sphere* (1998). Steven Spielberg directed the blockbuster, which starred Sam Neill as Dr. Alan Grant, Laura Dern as Dr. Ellie Sattler, Jeff Goldblum as Dr. Ian Malcolm, and Richard Attenborough as John Hammond.

An all-star cast, groundbreaking special effects, and a gripping story virtually assured that *Jurassic Park* would be a hit at the box office. A good deal of the movie's success was due to director Steven Spielberg, who brought Crichton's vision to the big screen. *Jurassic Park* was the top-grossing movie of 1993, eventually earning nearly $1 billion. The budget for making the film was high for the time, at roughly $63 million.

After the movie's release, interest in paleontology, especially in dinosaurs, exploded. People wanted more information on how and where dinosaurs lived and why they became extinct. Toys, action figures, posters, T-shirts, books, board games, and other souvenirs appeared, all with the familiar red and black *Jurassic Park* logo. Universal Studios opened *Jurassic Park* rides at their theme parks. *Jurassic Park* videos, DVDs, and video games brought in even more money.

Audiences had never seen anything like *Jurassic Park*'s realistic dinosaurs, and they wanted more. Two sequels have been made: *The Lost World: Jurassic Park* (1997) and *Jurassic Park III* (2001). A third sequel is planned for the series.

THE STORY OF *HONEY, I SHRUNK THE KIDS* (1989)

Wayne Szalinski is a kind husband and father who is building a miniaturization machine in his attic. While he's away at a scientific convention, the boy who lives next door hits a baseball into the Szalinski attic. It bounces onto the shrink machine, causing rays of energy to shoot out. The Szalinski children, Nick and Amy, plus the two neighbor boys, Russ and Ron, go up to the attic to get the baseball and are struck by the rays. They immediately shrink to the size of pinheads.

Szalinski comes home to his attic laboratory, disappointed that no one at the conference believes his theories. He beats the shrink machine with a baseball bat, sweeps up the pieces into a trash bag and takes the trash bag outside. Unbeknownst to Szalinksi, he has swept his children into the bag, too.

Outside by the alley, the children open the trash bag and get out. They realize they must cross the yard to get back to their house. Unless they can get their father to understand what happened, they may never return to normal size. They are so tiny that crossing the yard becomes a difficult journey, and they meet one obstacle after another.

Meanwhile, Szalinski figures out what has happened when he discovers that his couch has been shrunk. He searches for the children but cannot find them. The children manage to get onto the kitchen table where Szalinski is about to have breakfast. His son Nick falls into the cereal bowl and is scooped up into a

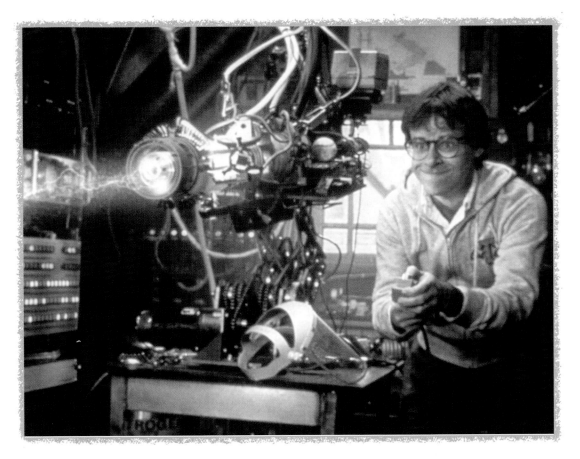

The machine invented by Dr. Wayne Szalinksi (Rick Moranis) to miniaturize matter in *Honey, I Shrunk the Kids* doesn't seem to work—until the children get in the way of its beam. In the film, it takes the tiny children two days to get across their backyard and home. Rick Moranis would star in several sequels to the original movie.

spoon. "Dad!" he screams. Szalinski sees him just in time and restores the children to their normal size.

THE COMIC MAD SCIENTIST

Released in 1989, *Honey, I Shrunk the Kids* was one of the most popular comedies of the year. The first major film by director

Joe Johnston, it starred Rick Moranis as the clueless Szalinski. It had none of the dark overtones of many mad scientist films and was instead a lighthearted look at the chaos new technology can create. *Honey, I Shrunk the Kids* showed a kind of mad scientist who isn't evil. Instead, Wayne Szalinksi is gentle, bumbling, and harmless. Usually, comic mad scientists have only good intentions. They are often friendly eccentrics who simply cannot control their experiments.

CHAPTER 3

THE LEGEND OF THE MAD SCIENTIST

The first mad scientist movie was made less than a century ago, but the legend of the mad scientist can be traced back to the ancient Greek myth of Prometheus. Prometheus stole fire from the gods and gave it to human beings, who were not meant to have it. Fire allowed humans to cook food, forge metal, and build weapons. Prometheus, however, was punished for daring to defy the gods.

Throughout the ages, this ancient story has inspired other legends, novels, plays, and other works of art, which became the forerunners of mad scientist movies.

THE LEGEND OF DR. FAUST

During the Middle Ages in Europe, a time when few people could read and write, the thirst for knowledge seemed suspicious to many people. The powerful Catholic Church would not tolerate any ideas about the universe that contradicted its strict teachings. Those who wanted to become educated,

In this early seventeenth-century woodcut, Dr. Faust conjures up the devil. Although this woodcut shows Faust standing inside a circle marked with symbols to protect himself, he ultimately ends up losing his soul. According to legend, Faust was so determined to learn the world's secrets he agreed to sell his own soul to the devil in exchange for knowledge and power.

especially those who experimented with chemistry, were sometimes suspected of having made bargains with the devil in order to gain forbidden knowledge. The legend of Dr. Faust embodied this fear.

Early in sixteenth-century Germany, stories were told about a mysterious man named Dr. Johann Faust. Thought to

be a magician and alchemist, Faust was said to have sold the devil his soul for power and knowledge. The legend of Faust endured over the years. In 1604, Christopher Marlowe wrote a play called *The Tragicall History of Dr. Faustus*, which made the evil doctor into a sympathetic character. In 1808, the first volume of the German poet Johann Wolfgang von Goethe's drama *Faust* was published; the second volume was published in 1832. The legend of Dr. Faust has served as a model for many mad scientist movies. Just like modern mad scientists, Dr. Faust's thirst for knowledge eventually led to his downfall. After Dr. Faust discovered the secrets of the universe, enjoyed the love of beautiful women, and traveled the world, the devil demanded his due: Faust's immortal soul.

ALCHEMISTS

In many versions of the Faust legend, Dr. Faust is an alchemist. Alchemists were early "scientists" who tried to gain wealth and immortality. One of the goals of alchemy was to make gold from other metals, such as lead. Anyone who could figure out how to make gold from a common metal like lead could become very rich and powerful.

Alchemists in ancient Egypt, Rome, China, Arabia, and medieval Europe experimented with various formulas to accomplish this. It was believed that a "philosopher's stone" could be found that would be used to transform metals into gold. Alchemists also tried to find a universal medicine that would cure every disease and perhaps even halt aging.

Although alchemy combined elements of chemistry and physics, it was not really a science. As the sciences became more developed, alchemy gradually faded away. With their strange laboratories, mysterious chemicals, and arcane practices, alchemists became the models for latter-day mad scientists.

ARTIFICIAL LIFE

In the movies, mad scientists often attempt to artificially create life. They assume that if they can create life and control their creations, they will have tremendous power. In Europe during the Middle Ages, it was thought that wizards and alchemists could make a homunculus from a mixture of human tissue and plant matter. A homunculus was believed to be a very tiny man. This creature was supposed to help and protect its creator but was not superhuman and did not have magical powers.

Another mythical man-made creature was the golem. In ancient Jewish legends, a golem was a creature made of clay or another inanimate substance. A rabbi could bring a golem to life by inscribing a sacred word on the golem's forehead.

In some legends, golems were robotlike creatures used primarily as servants. In other legends, a rabbi would create a golem to protect the community. The silent 1920 German film *The Golem* takes place in sixteenth-century Prague's Jewish ghetto. In the film, a rabbi creates a huge clay golem to save the Jews of Prague from brutal persecution. The golem wants to become human and rebels against being used as a servant. It eventually goes on a murderous rampage and has to be destroyed.

Stories about the golem are some of the earliest about man-made monsters, and forerunners of later robot stories. Above is a still from the silent film *The Golem,* which was released in 1920. In the movie, a golem is created to help protect people but then ends up harming them.

DR. VICTOR FRANKENSTEIN

One of the best-known mad scientists appeared in Mary Shelley's 1818 novel *Frankenstein, or the Modern Prometheus.* In the book, Dr. Victor Frankenstein wants to discover the secret of life. He creates a monster from the body parts of corpses and animates it. Although the monster is not evil at

The Bride of Frankenstein, the 1935 sequel to *Frankenstein*, is often considered to be as good as or better than the first movie. In the film, Dr. Frankenstein brings to life a dead woman to be a partner for the monster. The bride was played by actress Elsa Lanchester, who also portrayed a young Mary Shelley in the film.

first, it becomes infuriated when it realizes that human beings find it unnatural and horrifying. The monster goes on a killing spree, murdering Dr. Frankenstein's brother, best friend, and fiancée.

In some ways, the plot of Shelley's novel resembles the legend of the golem. Dr. Frankenstein creates a monster that he is unable to control and eventually attempts to destroy. However,

Dr. Frankenstein is not trying to create a creature that will protect his community. He is attempting to possess the secret of life. By attempting to "play God," he unleashes forces that he does not fully understand. Like Prometheus, he is punished for trying to steal knowledge that he is not meant to have.

Mary Shelley's story was adapted for the screen several times, but the most famous version of the story was made by Universal Studios in 1931. Directed by James Whale and starring Boris Karloff as the creature, *Frankenstein* became the blueprint for countless mad scientist movies that followed.

THE ATOMIC THREAT

As people's fears about science and technology have changed over the years, so have mad scientist films. One of the biggest changes in mad scientist films came with the beginning of the second World War. World War II (1939–1945) was the largest military conflict in history, involving dozens of countries and resulting in millions of deaths. The United States fought in the war against the Axis powers, which included Germany, Japan, and Italy. In 1945, the United States dropped atomic bombs on the Japanese cities of Hiroshima and Nagasaki.

It was the first time that atomic weapons had been used in combat, and they caused tremendous destruction. Over 100,000 people lost their lives in the initial blasts, and thousands more died from radiation sickness in the months and years that followed. It was discovered that atomic radiation can cause mutations in human and animal genes. These mutations can result in birth defects and cancerous tumors. People all over the world were terrified by the horrific destruction caused by atomic weapons.

Many mad scientist movies made during the 1950s underscored the public's fear of atomic radiation. A number of movies featuring monsters that were created or awakened by atomic weapons were made during this time. The most famous of these is *Them!* (1954), which features ants that become gigantic after being exposed to radiation. The giant ants spread across the American Southwest, finally ending up in Los Angeles, where they are destroyed by the U.S. military.

Movies such as *Them!* showed a different side of science and scientists. Instead of being all-powerful and evil, scientists in these movies are often ordinary people trying to save others from the horrors that science has created.

CHAPTER 4

MAD EFFECTS

There is always a creeping sense of inevitability in mad scientist movies, and it always seems that the mad scientist's work cannot be stopped. The audience knows from the first scene that the mad scientist will be punished or killed.

Special effects help bring mad scientists' insane experiments to life. They create the illusion of danger and make the audience believe that something unbelievable is happening.

EARLY EFFECTS

The special effects in early mad scientist movies were primitive by today's standards. Because they were working with basic technology, the filmmakers had to be very inventive in the way they made their special effects. By using lighting, makeup, and careful editing, these filmmakers created effects that kept the audience spellbound.

The transformation scene in 1931's *Dr. Jekyll and Mr. Hyde* was one of the film's most striking. Dr. Jekyll slowly turns into Mr. Hyde in front of the audience. During the filming of the black-and-white movie, Fredric

March wore brightly colored Hyde makeup in the scenes where he transformed into Hyde. On screen, the colorful Hyde makeup was hidden by red and green filters on the camera lens. To make him transform into his alter ego, the filters were gradually removed to reveal Hyde's face.

In *The Invisible Man*, director James Whale used wires to manipulate objects that were being "moved" by the invisible Dr. Griffin. While these movements were not always believable, Whale did manage to create some amazing effects for the movie. For a scene in which Dr. Griffin removes his bandages, Claude Rains dressed completely in black velvet and was filmed against a black velvet background. As his bandages dropped away, it appeared that there was nothing beneath.

TRANSFORMING INTO *THE FLY*

Makeup is an important part of frightening audiences in mad scientist movies. Chris Walas and Stephan Dupuis, the makeup artists for 1986's *The Fly*, won an Oscar for their work. *The Fly's* makeup was applied gradually during the filming of the movie, as Dr. Seth Brundle slowly turns into a monstrous insect. At first, his face looks strangely oily, then boils begin to spread over his skin. Eventually his ears fall off, his teeth drop out, and his fingers fuse together.

Jeff Goldblum had to spend up to five hours in the makeup chair as Walas and Dupuis applied latex and makeup to his face and body. Some of the most disgusting effects were accomplished with everyday materials: for instance, the substance

The special effects crew of *The Fly* came up with incredible effects to startle the audience. Special effects, especially makeup, must be done flawlessly to capture the belief of viewers. Sometimes, more time and money are spent on creating special effects than on the script. In this image, the special effects team manipulates a puppet of Seth Brundle in the final stages of his transformation.

that Brundle regurgitates on his food was made of honey, raw eggs, and milk. The special effects in *The Fly* were truly horrific, making it one of the most terrifying mad scientist movies ever made.

The accidentally shrunken Nick Szalinski, played by Robert Oliveri, swims in a milk-filled cereal bowl, shouting for help and desperately trying to avoid his father's spoon in the 1989 movie *Honey, I Shrunk the Kids*. To accomplish this effect, Oliveri was submerged in what looks like milk, holding onto a huge piece of "cereal," which was probably made from Styrofoam.

SHRINKING PEOPLE

Models are frequently used in movies that have unusual settings. One way to create the illusion of small people moving about in a giant environment is to have them interact with huge props. In *Honey, I Shrunk the Kids*, giant prop pencils, spoons, cookies, and Lego blocks dwarf the children, making us believe they are tiny. In scenes where the shrunken children appear alongside normal-sized people, the two sets of actors were filmed separately. The footage was then meshed together in the editing room.

BRINGING DINOSAURS TO LIFE

The special effects for *Jurassic Park* were created by the company Industrial Light and Magic (ILM), which won an Academy Award for its work on the movie. Founded by George Lucas in 1975, ILM has created special effects for movies such as *Star Wars* (1977), *Terminator 2: Judgment Day* (1991), and *Harry Potter and the Sorcerer's Stone* (2001). If anyone could bring dinosaurs to life, ILM could.

At first the idea was to use huge models of animatronic dinosaurs with a technique called go-motion. Go-motion animation was an improved version of stop-motion animation, where a single frame of a model would be photographed, the model would be slightly moved, another frame would be photographed, and so on. When run in sequence, the frames gave the illusion of motion. Since it takes dozens of frames to make up one second of screen time, stop-motion animation is extremely time-consuming and results in jerky movements that do not look real.

In go-motion, mechanical rods are attached to models or puppets. The rods are programmed to move the puppets while the camera lens is open, saving the filmmakers time and allowing the model to move more realistically. A few dinosaur models were made for *Jurassic Park*, but because the models were so large—the Tyrannosaurus rex model weighed about 15,000 pounds (6,800 kilograms)—their movements did not look natural. Regular puppets ended up working well for some of the smaller dinosaurs. For instance, velociraptor puppets were used in the scene where the children are trapped in the kitchen. The puppets were radio-controlled by cables, and the puppeteers hid from the camera in the cabinets.

Finally, ILM decided to try making digital dinosaurs. Computer-generated imagery (CGI) had been used in only a few movies at that time. Steven Spielberg was afraid the dinosaurs would look like cartoons instead of living creatures. It took months to feed all the information into the computers, but the hard work paid off—the CGI dinosaurs looked more genuine than anyone could have imagined.

On a plain set called a blue screen, the actors were instructed to react to unseen creatures and act as if the dinosaurs were present. The background and the dinosaurs were added later. Despite *Jurassic Park*'s strong cast, the CGI dinosaurs were the real stars of the movie, especially the fast-moving, ten-foot-tall velociraptors.

By the time of the 1997 sequel, *The Lost World*, the techniques of model-building had advanced. Forty new dinosaurs were created for that movie and were installed with programmed hydraulic devices that allowed them to move faster and more precisely. CGI dinosaurs were also used in the film, but the models were just as important. In 2001, *Jurassic Park III* featured dinosaurs that were even more realistic. In this story, the dinosaurs had been left completely alone on an island for years and had changed and multiplied. Hundreds of dinosaurs of a dozen varieties ran free, and the computer graphics were so good that the digital dinosaurs were indistinguishable from the models.

A Tyrannosaurus rex threatens the scientists and children touring Jurassic Park during a downpour. The 1993 film was directed by Steven Spielberg, whose vision for fast-moving adventures with spectacular special effects and thunderous sound changed moviemaking. *Jurassic Park* marked the first time digital effects assumed such a prominent role in a Hollywood film.

THE IMPACT OF *JURASSIC PARK*

Jurassic Park signaled a change in the way special effects were filmed. Before *Jurassic Park*, CGI had been used sparingly in films and seldom looked realistic. *Jurassic Park* proved that digital effects could be made to look indistinguishable from real life. After seeing how remarkable the CGI dinosaurs looked, other filmmakers began using CGI for special effects as well. Digital effects are becoming so realistic that soon filmmakers may only be limited by their imaginations.

THE FUTURE OF THE MAD SCIENTIST

Some of the inventions that appeared in mad scientist movies over the past fifty years are X-rays and laser beams; both are common nowadays. Bringing the dead back to life with electricity, which seemed so horrifying in movies like *Frankenstein*, is now done every day with defibrillator paddles.

Over the past 100 years, mad scientist stories have changed from starring a single evil genius who tries to create or alter life, to showing that an impersonal force can also be evil, such as atomic radiation, pollution, or technology out of control. Villains today can be greedy corporations, heartless politicians, or runaway technology. From the time of *Dr. Jekyll and Mr. Hyde*, the role of the mad scientist has changed significantly. As long as people are unsettled by science and technology, there will be mad scientist films.

FILMOGRAPHY

Dr. Jekyll and Mr. Hyde (1931) Fredric March plays Dr. Jekyll, a scientist who discovers a chemical that will transform him into an evil monster.

The Invisible Man (1931) Claude Rains stars as Dr. Jack Griffin, a scientist who loses his mind after drinking a solution that makes him invisible.

Island of Lost Souls (1933) A mad scientist uses surgery to create hybrids of humans and animals, called manimals. He is eventually destroyed by his unnatural creations.

Dr. Cyclops (1940) A mad scientist in Peru uses radium to shrink people to one-fifth their normal size.

Them! (1954) Giant ants, the result of radiation experiments, invade a town and spread throughout the American Southwest.

Forbidden Planet (1956) A scientist named Dr. Morbius goes mad after experimenting with thinking machines.

The Nutty Professor (1963) A geeky college professor drinks a concoction that makes him attractive and charming.

X: The Man with the X-Ray Eyes (1963) Dr. James Xavier experiments with drugs to give himself X-ray vision. Unfortunately, his ability begins to drive him mad.

The Man with Two Brains (1983) This comedy stars Steve Martin as mad scientist who invents an unconventional form of brain surgery.

The Fly (1986) Scientist Seth Brundle invents teleportation pods. During teleportation, his genes become fused with those of a fly.

Honey, I Shrunk the Kids (1989) A bumbling scientist's miniaturization machine shrinks his kids.

Edward Scissorhands (1990) A mad scientist creates a man named Edward, giving him scissors in the place of hands.

Jurassic Park (1993) Dinosaurs are brought to life on an island park and wreak havoc.

GLOSSARY

alchemy An early, unscientific form of chemistry.

CGI (computer-generated imagery) A technique that uses three-dimensional digital images to create special effects in movies.

convention A familiar plot or narrative device used in movies or literature.

DNA A substance found in the cells of living creatures that carries genetic information.

eccentric Having an unusual or odd personality.

homunculus A small, artificial, human-shaped creature, rumored to have been created by alchemists and wizards.

illusion A false perception, or something that deceives the senses.

Jurassic A geological period during which dinosaurs flourished.

mutation A change in the genetic structure of an organism.

nuclear radiation Invisible particles or waves emitted by radioactive substances. Nuclear radiation has been shown to cause mutations.

paleontology The study of fossils.

special effects Images and illusions in film that are created by technical means.

FOR MORE INFORMATION

American Film Institute
2021 N. Western Avenue
Los Angeles, CA 90027-1657
(323) 856-7600
Web Site: http://www.afi.com

WEB SITES

Due to the changing nature of Internet links, the Rosen
Publishing Group, Inc., has developed an online list of Web
sites related to the subject of this book. This site is updated
regularly. Please use this link to access the list:

http://www.rosenlinks.com/famm/masc

FOR FURTHER READING

Guttmacher, Peter. *Legendary Horror Films: Essential Genre History, Offscreen Anecdotes, Special Effects Secrets, Ghoulish Facts and Photographs.* New York, NY: Metrobooks, 1995.

Hamilton, Jake. *Special Effects in Film and Television.* New York, NY: DK Publishers, 1998.

Manchel, Frank. *An Album of Great Science Fiction Films.* New York, NY: Franklin Watts, 1982.

Palmer, Randy. *Paul Blaisdell, Monster Maker: A Biography of the B Movie Makeup and Special Effects Artist.* Jefferson, NC: McFarland, 1997.

Quakenbush, Robert. *Movie Monsters and Their Masters: The Birth of the Horror Film.* Chicago, IL: Albert Whitman, 1980.

Shay, Don, and Jody Duncan. *The Making of Jurassic Park.* New York, NY: Ballantine Books, 1993.

BIBLIOGRAPHY

Chapman, Douglas. "To a New World of Gods and Monsters: Mad Scientists and the Movies." Revision of "To a New World of Gods and Monsters: 'Mad' Scientists and the Movies." *Strange Magazine*, No. 2, 1988. Retrieved July 2005 (http://www.strangemag.com/madscientists/ madscientists.html).

Frank, Alan. *The Movie Treasury: Monsters and Vampires.* London, England: Octopus Books, 1976.

"Homunculus." Wikipedia. Retrieved July 2005 (http://en. wikipedia.org/wiki/Homunculus).

O'Connor, Jane, and Katy Hall. *Magic in the Movies: The Story of Special Effects*. New York: Doubleday, 1980.

Pinteau, Pascal. *Special Effects: An Oral History*. Translated by Laurel Hirsch. New York: Harry N. Abrams, 2005.

Shay, Don, and Jody Duncan. *The Making of* Jurassic Park. New York: Ballantine Books, 1993.

INDEX

ABOUT THE AUTHOR

Betty Burnett is a longtime fan of mad scientist movies. When she was growing up in Dallas, Texas, she went to the Saturday matinee at a movie theater almost every week. For only twenty-five cents, she could see two movies and several cartoons. Now she lives in St. Louis, Missouri, and watches DVDs on her computer.

PHOTO CREDITS

Cover, pp. 1, 9, 17, 29 © Everett Collection; pp. 4, 5, 7, 10, 16, 25, 26, 30, 33, © Bettmann/Corbis; p. 13 © 20th Century Fox Film Corp. All rights reserved. Courtesy Everett Collection; pp. 20, 39 © Close Murray/Corbis/Sygma; pp. 23, 36 © Buena Vista Pictures/Courtesy Everett Collection; p. 35 © Photofest.

Designer: Thomas Forget